CLIMATE CHANGE
iN THE TROPiCS

STUART BAKER

Marshall Cavendish
Benchmark

New York

This edition first published in 2010 in the United States of America
by Marshall Cavendish Benchmark.

Marshall Cavendish Benchmark
99 White Plains Road
Tarrytown, NY 10591
www.marshallcavendish.us

All Internet sites were available and accurate when sent to press.

First published in 2009 by
MACMILLAN EDUCATION AUSTRALIA PTY LTD
15–19 Claremont Street, South Yarra 3141

Visit our website at www.macmillan.com.au or go directly to www.macmillanlibrary.com.au

Associated companies and representatives throughout the world.

Copyright © Stuart Baker 2009

Library of Congress Cataloging-in-Publication Data

Baker, Stuart.
   In the tropics / by Stuart Baker.
       p. cm. – (Climate change)
   ISBN 978-0-7614-4440-4
   1. Tropics–Juvenile literature. I. Title.
   G907.B37 2010
   508.313–dc22

                              2009005768

Edited by Sally Woollett
Text and cover design by Christine Deering
Page layout by Christine Deering
Illustrations by Richard Morden
Photo research by Legend Images

Printed in the United States

Acknowledgments
The author and the publisher are grateful to the following for permission to reproduce
copyright material:

Front cover photograph: King tides hit Funafuti Atoll, 2004, courtesy of Torsten Blackwood/AFP/
Getty Images
Photos courtesy of:
© Flatscreen/Dreamstime.com, 10; © Christopher Waters/Fotolia, 11; Getty Images, 19; Torsten
Blackwood/AFP/Getty Images, 23 (bottom); Sebastian D'Souza/AFP/Getty Images, 14; Ove
Hoegh-Guidberg/AFP/Getty Images, 17; Mike Goldwater/Getty Images, 25; Christopher Pillitz/
Getty Images, 22; Kevin Schafer/Getty Images, 29 (bottom); © Travis Daub/iStockphoto, 18;
© Alexander Hafemann/iStockphoto, 21; © Chad Purser/iStockphoto, 15; NASA/Goddard
Space Flight Center, Scientific Visualization Studio, 24; NOAA CCMA Biogeography Team, 16;
Photolibrary © Ricardo Funari/BrazilPhotos/Alamy, 29 (top); Photolibrary © Ashley Cooper/
Alamy, 23 (top); Photolibrary © imagebroker/Alamy, 30; Photolibrary/David Kirkland, 13;
Photolibrary/Caroline Penn, 9; Photolibrary/Andy Who/SPL, 27

1 3 5 6 4 2

Contents

Glossary Words   When a word is printed in **bold**, you can look up its meaning in the Glossary on page 31.

Climate Change

Earth has been warming and cooling for millions of years. During the **Ice Age**, large areas of Europe and Canada were covered with **glaciers**. Earth's climate was 5.4–9°Fahrenheit (3–5°Celsius) cooler than it is today. The most recent Ice Age ended 20,000 years ago.

Rising Temperatures

Temperatures across the world are rising at a rate faster than ever before. Earth's average temperature has risen by 1.08°F (0.6°C) in the past one hundred years. The ten hottest years on record occurred over the past fourteen years. The hottest year ever recorded was 2005. This **global warming** may be enough to cause changes in weather patterns, which is commonly referred to as **climate change**.

Earth's Climate Zones

Earth can be divided into four main types of climate zones:

- Arctic

- Temperate

- Tropical

- Antarctic

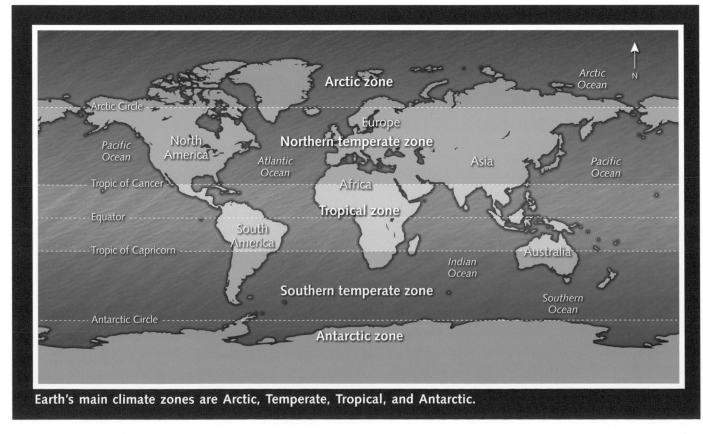

Earth's main climate zones are Arctic, Temperate, Tropical, and Antarctic.

The Tropics Region

The tropics region is centered on the **equator.** The tropics extend north to the Tropic of Cancer and south to the Tropic of Capricorn. These two lines of **latitude** are 23.5 degrees from the equator.

Large areas of Africa, Central and South America, and Southeast Asia lie within the tropics.

Climate

The tropics do not have four seasons as in other parts of the world. This is because the sun is overhead all year, resulting in consistent warm to hot conditions. At the equator, the hot conditions are accompanied by high humidity and regular rainfall, though there may also be a heavier wet season.

When people think of the tropics they often think of hot and wet conditions. Tropical weather conditions occur around the equator where rain forests are the main **ecosystem**. Other ecosystems within the tropics include deserts, grasslands, and coral reefs. Most of the world's hot deserts are found around the tropics of Cancer and Capricorn.

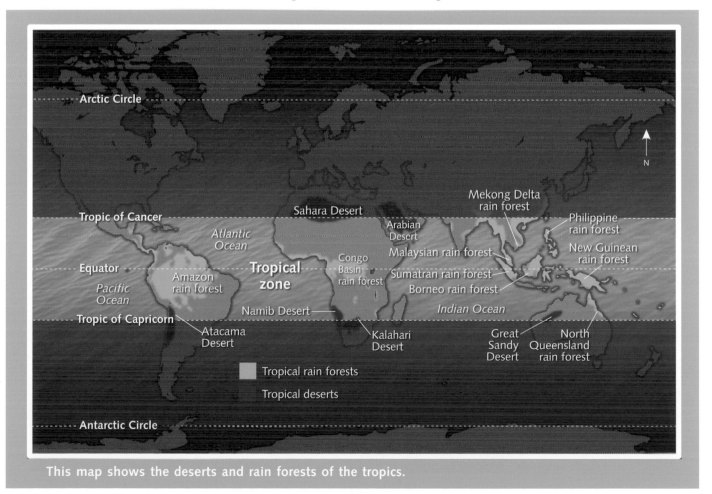

This map shows the deserts and rain forests of the tropics.

Global Warming and Greenhouse Gases

Global warming is caused by the **greenhouse effect**. **Greenhouse gases** trap the heat from the sun in Earth's **atmosphere**. This heat leads to an increase in Earth's surface temperature.

Greenhouse Gases

Greenhouse gases occur naturally in Earth's atmosphere, but human activities contribute to these gases. These human activities are increasing as the world's population increases.

Scientists now agree that in recent decades the amount of greenhouse gases in the atmosphere has increased. More of the sun's heat is being trapped, leading to further global warming. The term "global warming" in this book refers to the effects of this extra heat being trapped.

The Impact of Human Activities

Human activities generate three main greenhouse gases: **carbon dioxide**, **methane**, and **nitrous oxide**. Carbon dioxide is produced when **fossil fuels** such as coal and oil are burned. The level of carbon dioxide in the air is also affected by the clearing of forests, as trees and other plants absorb carbon dioxide to produce oxygen, which is vital to life on Earth. Methane is produced naturally by livestock such as cows and sheep who release it as part of their digestive process. It is also produced when substances such as manure and waste products in landfills begin to ferment, or turn sour. Nitrous oxide is produced when certain fertilizers are used to grow crops.

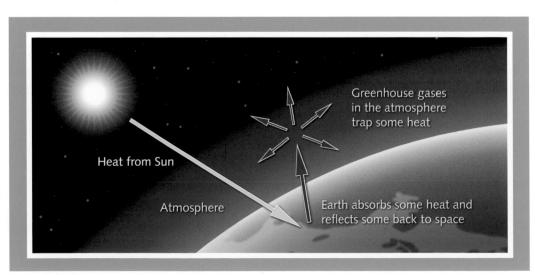

The greenhouse effect is the trapping of the Sun's heat due to certain gases in the atmosphere.

Heat from Sun

Greenhouse gases in the atmosphere trap some heat

Atmosphere

Earth absorbs some heat and reflects some back to space

Possible Effects of Global Warming

Scientists are making predictions about the effects of global warming. Global warming could affect the environment and humans in many different ways.

POSSIBLE EFFECTS OF GLOBAL WARMING IN THE TROPICS

POSSIBLE EVENT	PREDICTED RESULT	IMPACT ON THE TROPICS
EXTREME WEATHER EVENTS	✳ More frequent and severe hurricanes	✳ Greater property damage and loss of life, and spread of disease
CORAL BLEACHING	✳ Destruction of areas of coral	✳ Decline in the number of tourists visiting tropical reefs
SPREADING DRY ZONES	✳ Increased **desertification** as desert areas expand ✳ More drought conditions	✳ Loss of farmland ✳ Famine conditions due to food and water shortages
RISING SEA LEVELS	✳ Flooding	✳ Forced relocation of people in many tropical low-lying coastal cities and farmlands
CHANGES IN TEMPERATURE AND MOISTURE	✳ Breeding difficulties for **amphibians** ✳ Drier rain forests ✳ More favorable breeding conditions for mosquitoes	✳ Extinction of some species ✳ Loss of **biodiversity** ✳ Spreading of diseases such as malaria

Climate Change in the Tropics

By the year 2100 temperatures in the tropics are expected to be 3.6–5.4°F (2–3°C) higher than they are now. This is a small increase compared to the 10°F (6°C) or more increase predicted for the polar regions. However, as the tropics experience high temperatures all year, a relatively small change in temperature is likely to have a big impact on plants and animals that are adapted to tropical conditions.

Expanding Tropics

Global warming has caused changes in the tropics. Subtropical dry regions have expanded toward the poles by 183 miles (295 kilometers) over the past twenty-five years. The drier conditions are already being noticed in South Africa and Australia, and in Mediterranean countries such as Spain and Italy.

Fact ZONE

Up to one-third of Spain is in danger of turning into desert. Unrestricted tourism development and demands from farming are the main causes.

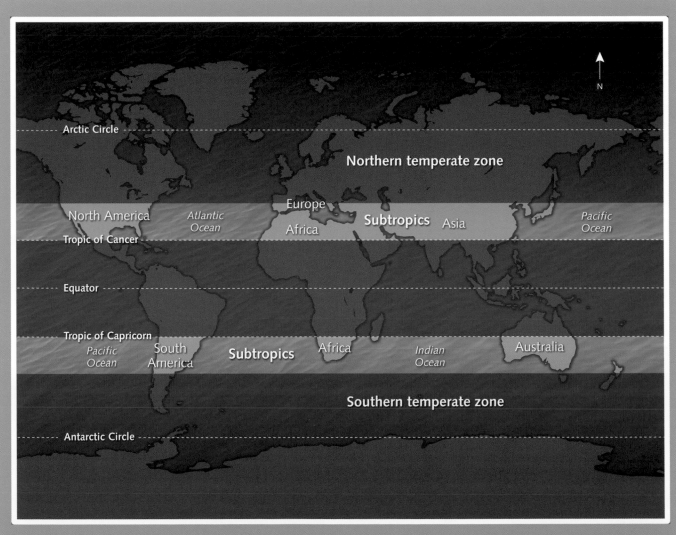

The subtropics lie above the Tropic of Cancer and below the Tropic of Capricorn, overlapping the temperate zones.

Food and Water Shortages

Increasing temperatures could have a major effect on farming and water supply in the tropics. A **United Nations** climate change group has warned that:

- up to 250 million people across Africa could face water shortages by 2020, partly because of low rainfall

- crop yields could increase by 20 percent in East Asia and Southeast Asia, but decrease by up to 30 percent in Central and South Asia

- the yields of very important crops such as rice, wheat, and maize are likely to drop by 10 percent for every 1.8°F (1°C) that temperature rises. (Increased temperature and greenhouse gases can damage the ability of crops to flower and reproduce.)

Most of the world's poor people live in the tropics. Their survival depends on farming. These changes could result in a food shortage. There are fears that if crop yields decline, farmers may be forced to clear rain forests in higher, cooler areas, which also support the rain forest environment. The clearing of these forests would cause further global warming and destroy wildlife **habitat**.

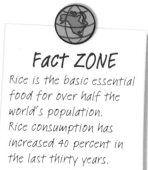

Fact ZONE
Rice is the basic essential food for over half the world's population. Rice consumption has increased 40 percent in the last thirty years.

Higher temperatures could mean more water shortages for many tropical countries. These women in Eritrea have to line up to receive their water rations.

The Natural World of the Tropics

Fact ZONE

Animals and plants have adapted to survive harsh desert conditions:

- Camels can survive for days without drinking water and can drink up to 22 gallons (100 liters) at a time.
- The creosote bush has an oily varnish on its leaves that seals in moisture.

Rainfall varies within the tropics. This means the tropics can support many different ecosystems, including:

- rain forests
- deserts
- savannas
- coral reefs

At the equator 13 to 26 feet (4–8 meters) of rain falls per year. Rain forests thrive in these hot, moist conditions, where temperatures rarely rise above 95°F (35°C) and rarely fall below 77°F (25°C). Most countries near the equator have tropical rain forests.

Many areas near the tropics of Cancer and Capricorn receive less than 10 inches (250 millimeters) of rain per year and have temperatures as high as 122°F (50°C). These include deserts such as the Sahara in Africa, the Atacama in South America, and the Great Sandy in Australia.

Parts of the tropics support savannas, and warmer seas of the region have developed coral reefs.

Deserts such as the Namib in Namibia are a harsh natural environment in the tropics.

Tropical Rain Forests

Tropical rain forests are home to more than half of the 5 million animal and plant species on Earth. This biodiversity makes rain forests one of the world's most important ecosystems.

About one-quarter of the medicines used today contain ingredients found in rain forests. Some of the plants in rain forests have medicinal properties that treat leukemia, some heart conditions, and arthritis. Seventy percent of plants that contain possible cures for cancer are found in rain forests.

Rain forests, such as this one in Thailand, are the richest ecosystems on Earth.

Tropical Rain Forests and Climate Control

Tropical rain forests have been called the "lungs of the world" because they produce large amounts of oxygen. They help to control Earth's climate by absorbing large amounts of carbon dioxide, a greenhouse gas. Plants in the rain forest use the carbon dioxide and make oxygen during the process of photosynthesis. In this process, rain forests release large amounts of oxygen and a fine mist of water into the atmosphere.

Fact ZONE
The largest area of rain forest is the Amazon in South America. It covers more than 2.3 million square miles (6 million square kilometers), about three-quarters of the area of Australia.

Rain Forests

Background

Tropical rain forests are very wet and humid places. Many types of food grow in rain forests, such as bananas, avocados, coffee beans, corn, and pineapples.

In most climates, the water from rainfall evaporates and is carried away by the wind to fall as rain somewhere else. In rain forests such as the Amazon, however, most rain is a result of evaporation within the forest itself, which means the plants create their own rainfall. Water vapor is trapped by the canopy of the forest. Gentle winds lift the vapor higher into the atmosphere, where they cool, form clouds, and eventually fall as rain again.

Rain forests are divided into four main layers. The top layer is called the emergent layer. Trees that fall within this layer usually grow above the canopy of the rain forest and can reach heights of more than 148 ft (45 m). The canopy is the "roof" of the rain forest, where trees grow to heights between 98 and 131 ft (30–40 m). The layer below the canopy is known as the understory. This is where most of the rain forest's wildlife can be found. The final layer is the ground cover, or forest floor. Very little sunlight reaches this layer, which means not many plants can grow there.

Fact ZONE

Rain forests are disappearing rapidly. An area the same size as two football fields is cleared every second.

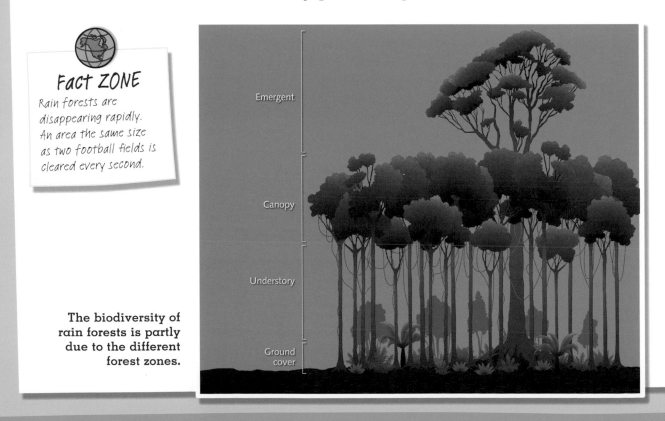

Emergent

Canopy

Understory

Ground cover

The biodiversity of rain forests is partly due to the different forest zones.

Drying Rain Forests

Plants release less water when carbon dioxide levels in the atmosphere increase. This could mean less precipitation in rain forest regions. Higher temperatures and lower rainfall may cause rain forests to become drier. This could eventually destroy rain forest ecosystems.

Climate change could result in up to two-thirds of the Amazon rain forest becoming savanna. This would have a big impact on biodiversity. Animals that have adapted to living in the rain forest would struggle to survive in the more open grasslands of the savanna.

Loss of the rain forest would expose soil to the atmosphere. Soil contains carbon dioxide produced by rotting vegetation such as fallen leaves. This carbon dioxide is released more quickly from the soil when rain forests are cleared because the soil is exposed to more oxygen in the air. Oxygen helps the rotting vegetation to decompose faster.

Clouds of mist form over this tropical rain forest in Brunei.

Weather

Background

The water in the tropics is warm. Warm seas and oceans can influence the atmosphere above, sometimes causing extreme weather events such as hurricanes.

Hurricanes are the same type of weather event as typhoons or cyclones. The name depends on the ocean in which they form.

Climate change has increased the frequency of extreme weather events in the tropics. Heavier rain has caused bigger floods, and longer dry spells have caused worse droughts in some regions.

In 2005 Mumbai, India, received more than 3 feet (1 m) of rain in twenty-four hours.

Rising Sea Temperatures

Global warming has increased water temperatures in the tropics. Global sea levels will continue to rise because as oceans get warmer they expand.

Warm seas have a warming effect on the air. Warm air can hold more moisture than cool air, which can produce storms of great power.

Bigger and More Frequent Hurricanes

Since 1994 the number of severe hurricanes has doubled. A recent study found that an increase in temperature of 0.9°F (0.5°C) in the Atlantic Ocean resulted in a 40 percent increase in hurricane activity in the area. Furthermore, the hurricane season is extending, and each hurricane lasts for a longer period.

Rising sea levels mean higher storm surges and more coastal flooding, even from relatively minor hurricanes. Storms and strong winds cause flooding, property damage, financial hardship, and large numbers of injuries.

This house in New Orleans suffered major damage by Hurricane Katrina in 2005.

Coral Reefs

Background

Coral polyps, or corals, are marine animals (related to jellyfish) which usually have a protective skeleton around them. They feed on plankton, which are very tiny plants and animals that float near the surface of the sea. Corals get their beautiful colors from algae which live in their tissue. The algae, which need sunlight to survive, and coral depend on each other for different nutrients.

When thousands of corals group together, they form a coral reef. A single reef may contain up to three thousand different coral species. Coral reefs are one of the most productive ecosystems, supporting 25 percent of all marine fish.

Fact ZONE
In 1998 the second hottest year on record, the world lost an estimated 16 percent of its coral reefs.

Coral reefs are found in oceans around the tropics with a water temperature of 70 to 86°F (21–30°C). Rising sea temperatures are a severe threat to corals because when oceans get too warm the corals become stressed.

Coral reefs provide a habitat for many marine plant and animal species.

Coral Bleaching

When the water is too warm, corals become stressed and eject the algae which live with them. As the algae give corals their color, corals appear white once the algae is gone. This change, known as bleaching, is a warning signal that the coral reef is about to die. If temperatures return to normal the coral can recover. However, if temperatures remain high the coral will slowly die.

Another possible effect of global warming on reefs is rising sea levels. A higher sea level means the coral reefs will receive less sunlight, which they need to survive.

Coral bleaching occurs when ocean temperatures rise.

CASE STUDY

Great Barrier Reef

The Great Barrier Reef extends for 1,429 miles (2,300 km) along the east coast of Queensland, Australia. It is the largest coral reef on Earth. Fishing and tourism generate 9.8 billion dollars each year. Some climate experts predict that at the current rate of global warming only 5 percent of the reef will remain by 2050. In addition to coral bleaching, the reef is threatened by severe tropical storms, which can break up the coral. Flooding events on the mainland can disturb fine soil particles that have settled at the bottom of rivers and flush them out to sea and onto the coral. As a result, this film of sediment blocks the Sun's rays from reaching the coral and the algae within it.

The impact of climate change on...

Amphibians

Background

Amphibians can live both on the land and in water. They include frogs, toads, newts, and salamanders.

Amphibians are most diverse in the tropics, including rain forests. Brazil has 789 species of amphibians.

One-third of the world's species of amphibians, around 1,800 species, are threatened by extinction.

Fact ZONE

The poison dart frog is brightly colored to ward off predators. The poison it produces is used by **indigenous** people of the Amazon rain forest to poison their darts and arrows.

Climate change is likely to have a direct impact on amphibian habitats. As temperatures increase and weather extremes, such as storms, floods, and drier conditions occur more frequently, changes in weather patterns can change amphibian breeding behavior and affect breeding success.

Global warming has been suggested as a reason for the decline in the number of salamanders, particularly in Central America.

Breeding Problems

Amphibians are extremely sensitive to small changes in temperature and moisture. If climate changes occur very quickly, some species may not survive.

During the breeding season, amphibians need enough water for tadpoles to survive and grow into adults. Increased temperatures cause the rain clouds to form higher in the atmosphere, above the canopy of the rain forest. As a result, forests once covered in mist are drying out and there are fewer water sources for breeding.

The golden toad is thought to be extinct because of global warming.

CASE STUDY

Golden Toad

Climate change has already led to the extinction of the golden toad. This small shiny toad was only found in a small area of high cloud-covered forest above Monteverde, Costa Rica, In Central America. Around 1,500 toads were sighted in 1987 but none have been seen since 1989. The toads rely on seasonal pools of water in which to lay their eggs. Unfortunately, warmer sea surface temperatures have resulted in lower rainfall and drier conditions in the cloud forests. Without the pools of water at the time of breeding, few tadpoles survive to adulthood.

Humans in the Tropics

More than three-quarters of the world's population live within the tropics. Six of the ten most populated, developing countries are located there as well.

Poverty and Pressure for Farmland

Many of the people who live in the tropics have little food and access to good medical care. Most people in these poor countries earn a living from farming and the growing population puts added strain on the land.

In Brazil, which has a rapidly growing population, the government has allowed large areas of rain forest to be farmed. New settlers have been moving into the rain forest and clearing it to raise cattle.

Ten most populated countries (2007)

Country	Population
China	1.3 billion
India*	1.1 billion
United States	301 million
Indonesia*	234 million
Brazil*	190 million
Pakistan*	169 million
Bangladesh*	150 million
Russia	141 million
Nigeria*	135 million
Japan	127 million

* Located in the tropics.

Movement to the Cities

Many people in the tropics have moved from rural areas into cities to find work to support themselves and their families. Unfortunately, most of the cities cannot accommodate the extra people. Poorer people often live in makeshift communities, usually located far from the city center, on steep slopes or near industrial land. They lack basic services such as sewers, running water, and electricity. Many homes are made from whatever materials are available.

The standard of living of most of the people who live in developing areas such as Borneo is low.

Indigenous People

About a thousand groups of indigenous people have lived in rain forest areas for thousands of years. They hunt wild animals and gather plant foods from the forest. They have great knowledge of the forest and know how to look after it in a sustainable way. Groups like the Penan of Borneo and the Yanomani Indians of Brazil are threatened by rain forest destruction.

The impact of climate change on...

Coastal Areas

Background

Many major cities are located along coastlines. Flat coastal plains helped these cities to expand as motorways and railroad tracks were easier to construct, enabling trade and communication. Harbor development was another factor, especially back when these cities were founded, as most goods were transported by ship.

Flat coastal plains are often also associated with the lower courses of rivers, where fertile land can be found. This encourages intensive farming, which supports a growing population.

Fact ZONE
Climate experts view rising sea levels as the greatest danger posed by global warming.

When water is warmer it expands, leading to higher sea levels. Sea levels are rising as a result of warmer sea temperatures and melting ice. The effects of rising sea levels pose a threat to low-lying coastal locations. In Bangladesh, in tropical Asia, rising sea levels would cause the flooding of vast areas of farmland and lead to food shortages and force millions of people to move.

Many ports and coastal towns in Bangladesh will be flooded if sea levels continue to rise.

Warmer Seas

Global sea levels have already increased 4 to 8 inches (10–20 cm) during the last century due to global warming. Any increase in sea levels due to global warming in the tropics is likely to be gradual. Governments will have time to develop coastal defenses to prevent flooding or move people away. Major flooding of coastal cities would mean relocating homes, industry, and transportation systems.

Melting Ice

A United Nations climate change panel has stated that a temperature increase of 5.4°F (3°C), predicted to occur by 2100, would cause the Greenland ice sheet to start melting. This would cause a 3-ft (1 m) rise in sea levels, and levels would continue to rise by 3 ft (1 m) every one hundred years.

CASE STUDY

Tuvalu

Tuvalu, a group of nine small islands in the Pacific Ocean, is at the front line of climate change.

The highest point on the islands is only 15 feet (4.5 m) above sea level. Increasingly severe storms and rising sea levels are already having an impact. Frequent flooding of gardens reduces the ability to grow food and also pollutes the freshwater supply. Fish catches have dropped due to damaged coral habitats. Although Tuvalu will not be submerged immediately, the population may need to be moved in the future.

The low-lying islands of Tuvalu are threatened by global warming.

Flooding causes many problems in Tuvalu, including pollution.

Desertification

Background

Desert areas receive less than 10 inches (250 millimeters) of rain per year and cover one-fifth of the Earth's land surface.

Deserts are often thought to be lifeless areas but are home to plants and animals able to survive the harsh conditions.

People who live in the desert struggle to live by farming crops such as millet and sorghum, and by raising cattle and sheep.

Climate change is causing longer periods of drought in farming areas at the edges of many of the world's deserts. Once-productive farmland is being turned into nonproductive desert. This process is known as desertification. Wind is blowing away valuable farming soil.

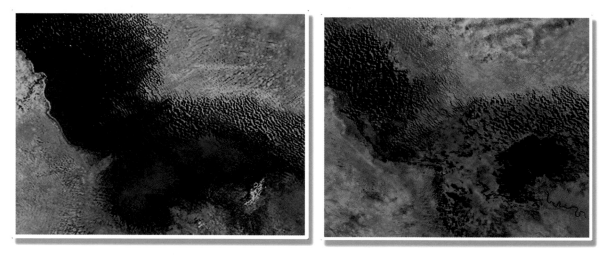

Lake Chad, which lies in the Sahel region of Africa, has been severely affected by droughts. Decreasing rainfall has seen the size of the lake drop to one-twentieth of its size, as seen here in images taken in 1973 (left) and 2001 (right).

Desertification

More severe and frequent droughts could increase desertification. One-third of Earth's land surface is threatened by desertification, and over 250 million people are directly affected. The areas worst affected are Africa, Asia, and Latin America, which include many tropical countries.

Soil Erosion

As areas become desert they have less plant material to hold the soil together. In windy conditions the valuable farming soil is blown away, a process called erosion. The land in semi-dry areas is usually poor and farming is difficult. Losing farming soil means the land can no longer support crops.

Poor soil in dry areas makes land difficult to farm.

CASE STUDY

Sahel Famine

Since the 1960s the Sahel has experienced long periods of below-average rainfall. The 1970s drought caused the deaths of over 300,000 people and 5 million livestock. In 2005 drought resulted in over one-quarter of Niger's population suffering hunger or starvation, including over 80,000 children. The United Nations and other organizations provided emergency food and medical supplies. New varieties of millet and sorghum that can survive drought are being grown and millions of trees have been planted to protect the soil from being lost.

Malaria

Background

Malaria is a disease that affects people in large areas of Africa, Southeast Asia, and South America. It occurs in hot tropical countries. An estimated 700,000 to 2.7 million people die of malaria each year, mostly African children.

Malaria is transmitted by a type of mosquito that carries a parasite in its saliva. When the mosquito bites an animal or human, it passes the parasite to them. They then develop malaria.

During the 1950s and 1960s malaria was decreasing because the disease was being controlled. Today, it is on the increase and research has linked this increase to climate change.

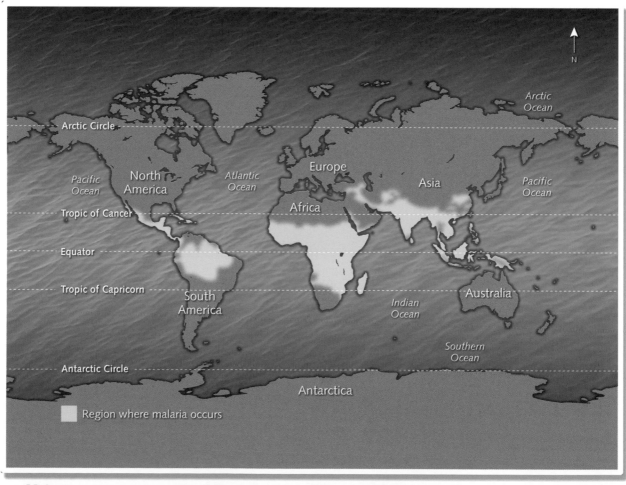

Malaria occurs across parts of South America, Africa, and Asia.

Malaria on the Increase

Malaria has been spreading to areas once too cold for mosquitoes, but which are now warmer. Research has shown that even a small increase in temperature can cause a ten-fold increase in mosquito populations.

Good Breeding Conditions

Climate change has not been the only factor in the spread of the mosquito. Clearing forests for farming has helped the mosquito by providing more favorable breeding conditions. Rapid population growth and poor access to health care are also making the situation worse.

Fact ZONE
Mosquitoes prefer children to adults and can smell humans 66 to 115 feet (20–35 m) away.

CASE STUDY

Mosquito Migration

The East African highlands are getting warmer. With higher temperatures, rainfall, and humidity, the mosquito has been able to migrate higher up the mountains. Approximately 220 to 400 million people live in the East African highlands and are now at risk of malaria. East Africa is an area of developing countries where health and health care are poor. Climate change will worsen the health situation for people in this area.

Mosquito nets protect sleeping people from malaria-carrying mosquitoes.

Taking Action on Climate Change

Many low-lying parts of the tropics are extremely vulnerable to global warming and climate change. The international community is working to understand and act on its impact.

Human activity is generally accepted as the main cause of global warming and climate change. Decreasing the amount of carbon dioxide and other greenhouse gases in the atmosphere is the best way to slow global warming.

Global Response

A total of 170 countries have signed the **Kyoto Protocol**. Industrialized, developed countries agreed to cut their combined greenhouse gas emissions to 5 percent below their 1990 level by 2012.

At the United Nations Climate Change Conference in Bali in 2007 delegates agreed to discuss a new climate change agreement to replace the Kyoto Protocol, which expires in 2012. These objectives were discussed further at the United Nations Framework Convention on Climate Change in Poznan, Poland, in December 2008. The purpose of the discussions was to set targets for future greenhouse gas reductions. Many scientists suggest that cuts of 60 percent are needed to avoid the worst consequences of global warming.

Fact ZONE

The United States, which has not signed the Kyoto Protocol, produces 20 percent of all greenhouse gases. Some people believe the Kyoto Protocol will have little effect.

CASE STUDY

The Kyoto Protocol

The Kyoto Protocol is an agreement between certain countries that sets targets to reduce greenhouse gas emissions. It was negotiated in Kyoto, Japan, in 1997.

Each country that has signed the Kyoto Protocol has agreed to its own particular target.

The United States is the only developed country that hasn't signed the agreement.

Countries such as China and India do not have to meet the emission targets because they have only recently begun to develop their industries. Other industrial countries have caused the current levels of greenhouse gases in the atmosphere to rise.

The Kyoto Protocol will be replaced by a new climate change agreement in 2012.

Carbon Trading and Developing Countries

Developing countries could earn more money from protecting their forests than they would by chopping them down. A country with acres of forests is removing a lot of carbon dioxide from the atmosphere. Some of these countries can earn **carbon credits**, which they can sell to countries struggling to meet their greenhouse gas targets. This is called carbon trading.

Brazilian Response: Biofuel

Brazil is leading the world in the production of ethanol, a **biofuel** that can be produced from sugar cane. Most cars in Brazil now run on ethanol or a combination of ethanol and petrol. A car using ethanol returns to the atmosphere the carbon dioxide absorbed by growing sugar cane plants.

Sugar cane, an important source of biofuel in Brazil, is processed in big factories such as this one, before being loaded onto trucks for transportation.

Community Response: Ecotourism

In Costa Rica, in Central America, local communities have recognized that many tourists want to visit rain forests because of their biodiversity. Preserving the forest in national parks for ecotourism, where visitors can enjoy the rain forest without damaging it, is now recognized as being of greater long-term benefit to the local community than destroying it.

Ecotourism in countries such as Costa Rica may help preserve the rain forest and its biodiversity.

The Future

Rising sea levels, severe weather events, and desertification are predicted due to climate change in the tropics. This may result in increased disease, and loss of property and food supplies.

Protecting Rain Forests

Today, there is a greater awareness of the link between rain forests and climate change. Protecting rain forests in the tropics slows global warming by:

- helping to reduce the amount of greenhouse gas entering the atmosphere by absorbing carbon dioxide

- locking up large amounts of carbon, which would otherwise be released to the atmosphere as forests are burned

Many people in tropical developing countries depend on farming to survive. Some developed countries are assisting people in these countries so that they don't need to clear the rain forests to grow food. In this way the rain forests are protected and can help to control global warming in the future.

Forests in Paraguay have been cleared at an alarming rate to make way for crop farming, as shown here.

amphibian	an animal spending part of its life in water and part on the land
atmosphere	the layer of gases that surrounds Earth
biodiversity	the wide variety of plants and animals living on Earth
biofuel	a renewable fuel made from plant material such as corn
carbon credits	financial rewards for activities that reduce levels of carbon dioxide in the atmosphere
carbon dioxide	a greenhouse gas produced by burning fossil fuels and clearing forests
climate change	changes in weather patterns caused by global warming
desertification	the process of change from useable land, such as farmland, into desert
ecosystem	a group of living things and their habitat
equator	an imaginary line that circles Earth and lies exactly halfway between the North and South poles
extinction	the death of every member of a group of living things
fossil fuel	a fuel such as coal or oil made of fossilized remains of plants
glaciers	slow-moving frozen rivers of ice
global warming	an increase in the average surface temperature of Earth
greenhouse effect	the warming of Earth's surface due to trapping of heat by the atmosphere
greenhouse gas	a gas that helps trap the sun's heat in the atmosphere
habitat	the surroundings in which an animal or plant lives
Ice Age	a period when temperatures were lower and large areas of Earth were ice-covered
indigenous	native to an area
Kyoto Protocol	a special guideline that was created with the aim of reducing greenhouse gases
latitude	a measurement, in degrees, of the distance of a point from the equator
methane	a greenhouse gas produced by cattle and rotting plant material
nitrous oxide	a greenhouse gas produced from fertilizers
United Nations	a group of countries that have agreed to work together on matters such as peace, security, and cooperation

Index